THE DOER'S JOURNAL

For the process -driven doers

About the Doer's Journal:

Doers' Journal is designed for the focus requirements of a doer – meaning, Do-ers like *structure*, *order* and *routine* in their lives while also not wanting to get burnt out. As people who strongly believe in the power of *aggregated effort*, they require reminders and stability to repeat focus processes each day. The journal has a minimal, relaxed feel spaced out for breaks in between the entries and filled with fields for self evaluation so that the doers can adjust their processes as per results measured.

The Focus On What We Have:

"It's a funny thing about life, once you begin to take note of the things you are grateful for, you begin to lose sight of the things that you lack"
-Germany Kent

Meetings For This Quarter

	Mon	Tue	Wed	Thu	Fri	Sat	Sun
Week1							
Week2							
Week3							
Week4							
Week5							
Week6							
Week7							
Week8							
Week9							
Week10							
Week11							
Week12							

Month 1 : Goals and Deliverables

Week 1 aspired target :
Week 2 aspired target :
Week 3 aspired target :
Week 4 aspired target :

Week 1 completed target :
Week 2 completed target :
Week 3 completed target :
Week 4 completed target :

Month 1 : Finances

Week 1 : savings :
Week 2 : savings :
Week 3 : savings :
Week 4 : savings :

Week 1 : expenditure :
Week 2 : expenditure :
Week 3 : expenditure :
Week 4 : expenditure :

Month 1 : Total investment:
Month 1 : Total growth :
Month 1 : Total Expenditure :
Month 1 : Average time to complete repeat task:
Month 1 : Average time for meditation/ workout:

Month 2 : Goals and Deliverables

Week 1 aspired target :
Week 2 aspired target :
Week 3 aspired target :
Week 4 aspired target :

Week 1 completed target :
Week 2 completed target :
Week 3 completed target :
Week 4 completed target :

Month 2 : Finances

Week 1 : savings :
Week 2 : savings :
Week 3 : savings :
Week 4 : savings :

Week 1 : expenditure :
Week 2 : expenditure :
Week 3 : expenditure :
Week 4 : expenditure :

Month 2 : Total investment:
Month 2 : Total growth :
Month 2 : Total Expenditure :
Month 2 : Average time to complete repeat task:
Month 2 : Average time for meditation/ workout:

Month 3 : Goals and Deliverables

Week 1 aspired target :
Week 2 aspired target :
Week 3 aspired target :
Week 4 aspired target :

Week 1 completed target :
Week 2 completed target :
Week 3 completed target :
Week 4 completed target :

Month 3 : Finances

Week 1 : savings :
Week 2 : savings :
Week 3 : savings :
Week 4 : savings :

Week 1 : expenditure :
Week 2 : expenditure :
Week 3 : expenditure :
Week 4 : expenditure :

Month 3 : Total investment:
Month 3: Total growth :
Month 3 : Total Expenditure :
Month 3: Average time to complete repeat task:
Month 3: Average time for meditation/ workout:

1.Self concept : Date:

What are your morning affirmations for today?

Physical:
Emotional:
Social:
Spiritual:

How well rested did you feel in the morning?

What are your plans, meetings, targets and non - negotiables for today? Check them out at the end of the day.

What are your key work hours today with breaks in between?

How did you manage distractions on phone/ email today?On average what was non- work related screen time today?

What physical activity or workout did you do today? Denote with mins or reps.

How much was spent out of pocket today? In what?

Was there any negotiation? Business, time and family? Write down 2 amazing things about you or about the way you think.

What insecurities and negative feelings did you deal with today? How do you rationalize them for tomorrow?

Draw a diagram/ art / flowchart of your dreams today: use intuition

What are your before-bed affirmations for today?
Physical:
Emotional:
Social:
Spiritual:

One new psycho - spiritual learning from you today:

2.Self concept : Date:

What are your morning affirmations for today?

Physical:
Emotional:
Social:
Spiritual:

How well rested did you feel in the morning?

What are your plans, meetings, targets and non - negotiables for today? Check them out at the end of the day.

What are your key work hours today with breaks in between?

How did you manage distractions on phone/ email today?On average what was non- work related screen time today?

What physical activity or workout did you do today write with mins or reps.

How much was spent out of pocket today? In what?

Was there any negotiation? Business, time and family? Write down 2 amazing things about you or about the way you think.

What insecurities and negative feelings did you deal with today? How do you rationalize them for tomorrow?

Draw a diagram/ art / flowchart of your dreams today: use intuition

What are your before-bed affirmations for today?
Physical:
Emotional:
Social:
Spiritual:

One new psycho - spiritual learning from you today:

3.Self concept : Date:

What are your morning affirmations for today?

Physical:
Emotional:
Social:
Spiritual:

How well rested did you feel in the morning?

What are your plans, meetings, targets and non - negotiables for today? Check them out at the end of the day.

What are your key work hours today with breaks in between?

How did you manage distractions on phone/ email today?On average what was non- work related screen time today?

What physical activity or workout did you do today write with mins or reps.

How much was spent out of pocket today? In what?

Was there any negotiation? Business, time and family? Write down 2 amazing things about you or about the way you think.

What insecurities and negative feelings did you deal with today? How do you rationalize them for tomorrow?

Draw a diagram/ art / flowchart of your dreams today: use intuition

What are your before-bed affirmations for today?

Physical:
Emotional:
Social:
Spiritual:

One new psycho - spiritual learning from you today:

4.Self concept : Date:

What are your morning affirmations for today?

Physical:
Emotional:
Social:
Spiritual:

How well rested did you feel in the morning?

What are your plans, meetings, targets and non - negotiables for today? Check them out at the end of the day.

What are your key work hours today with breaks in between?

How did you manage distractions on phone/ email today?On average what was non- work related screen time today?

What physical activity or workout did you do today? Denote with mins or reps.

How much was spent out of pocket today? In what?

Was there any negotiation? Business, time and family? Write down 2 amazing things about you or about the way you think.

What insecurities and negative feelings did you deal with today? How do you rationalize them for tomorrow?

Draw a diagram/ art / flowchart of your dreams today: use intuition

What are your before-bed affirmations for today?
Physical:
Emotional:
Social:
Spiritual:

One new psycho - spiritual learning from you today:

5.Self concept : Date:

What are your morning affirmations for today?

Physical:
Emotional:
Social:
Spiritual:

How well rested did you feel in the morning?

What are your plans, meetings, targets and non - negotiables for today? Check them out at the end of the day.

What are your key work hours today with breaks in between?

How did you manage distractions on phone/ email today?On average what was non- work related screen time today?

What physical activity or workout did you do today? Denote with mins or reps.

How much was spent out of pocket today? In what?

Was there any negotiation? Business, time and family? Write down 2 amazing things about you or about the way you think.

What insecurities and negative feelings did you deal with today? How do you rationalize them for tomorrow?

Draw a diagram/ art / flowchart of your dreams today: use intuition

What are your before-bed affirmations for today?
Physical:
Emotional:
Social:
Spiritual:

One new psycho - spiritual learning from you today:

6.Self concept : Date:

What are your morning affirmations for today?

Physical:
Emotional:
Social:
Spiritual:

How well rested did you feel in the morning?

What are your plans, meetings, targets and non - negotiables for today? Check them out at the end of the day.

What are your key work hours today with breaks in between?

How did you manage distractions on phone/ email today?On average what was non- work related screen time today?

What physical activity or workout did you do today? Denote with mins or reps.

How much was spent out of pocket today? In what?

Was there any negotiation? Business, time and family? Write down 2 amazing things about you or about the way you think.

What insecurities and negative feelings did you deal with today? How do you rationalize them for tomorrow?

23

Draw a diagram/ art / flowchart of your dreams today: use intuition

What are your before-bed affirmations for today?
Physical:
Emotional:
Social:
Spiritual:

One new psycho - spiritual learning from you today:

7.Self concept : Date:

What are your morning affirmations for today?

Physical:
Emotional:
Social:
Spiritual:

How well rested did you feel in the morning?

What are your plans, meetings, targets and non - negotiables for today? Check them out at the end of the day.

What are your key work hours today with breaks in between?

How did you manage distractions on phone/ email today?On average what was non- work related screen time today?

What physical activity or workout did you do today? Denote with mins or reps.

How much was spent out of pocket today? In what?

Was there any negotiation? Business, time and family? Write down 2 amazing things about you or about the way you think.

What insecurities and negative feelings did you deal with today? How do you rationalize them for tomorrow?

Draw a diagram/ art / flowchart of your dreams today: use intuition

What are your before-bed affirmations for today?
Physical:
Emotional:
Social:
Spiritual:

One new psycho - spiritual learning from you today:

8. Self concept : Date:

What are your morning affirmations for today?

Physical:
Emotional:
Social:
Spiritual:

How well rested did you feel in the morning?

What are your plans, meetings, targets and non - negotiables for today? Check them out at the end of the day.

What are your key work hours today with breaks in between?

How did you manage distractions on phone/ email today?On average what was non- work related screen time today?

What physical activity or workout did you do today? Denote with mins or reps.

How much was spent out of pocket today? In what?

Was there any negotiation? Business, time and family? Write down 2 amazing things about you or about the way you think.

What insecurities and negative feelings did you deal with today? How do you rationalize them for tomorrow?

Draw a diagram/ art / flowchart of your dreams today: use intuition

What are your before-bed affirmations for today?
Physical:
Emotional:
Social:
Spiritual:

One new psycho - spiritual learning from you today:

9.Self concept : Date:

What are your morning affirmations for today?

Physical:
Emotional:
Social:
Spiritual:

How well rested did you feel in the morning?

What are your plans, meetings, targets and non - negotiables for today? Check them out at the end of the day.

What are your key work hours today with breaks in between?

How did you manage distractions on phone/ email today?On average what was non- work related screen time today?

What physical activity or workout did you do today? Denote with mins or reps.

How much was spent out of pocket today? In what?

Was there any negotiation? Business, time and family? Write down 2 amazing things about you or about the way you think.

What insecurities and negative feelings did you deal with today? How do you rationalize them for tomorrow?

Draw a diagram/ art / flowchart of your dreams today: use intuition

What are your before-bed affirmations for today?
Physical:
Emotional:
Social:
Spiritual:

One new psycho - spiritual learning from you today:

10. Self concept : Date:

What are your morning affirmations for today?

Physical:
Emotional:
Social:
Spiritual:

How well rested did you feel in the morning?

What are your plans, meetings, targets and non - negotiables for today? Check them out at the end of the day.

What are your key work hours today with breaks in between?

How did you manage distractions on phone/ email today?On average what was non- work related screen time today?

What physical activity or workout did you do today? Denote with mins or reps.

How much was spent out of pocket today? In what?

Was there any negotiation? Business, time and family? Write down 2 amazing things about you or about the way you think.

What insecurities and negative feelings did you deal with today? How do you rationalize them for tomorrow?

Draw a diagram/ art / flowchart of your dreams today: use intuition

What are your before-bed affirmations for today?
Physical:
Emotional:
Social:
Spiritual:

One new psycho - spiritual learning from you today:

11 Self concept : Date:

What are your morning affirmations for today?

Physical:
Emotional:
Social:
Spiritual:

How well rested did you feel in the morning?

What are your plans, meetings, targets and non - negotiables for today? Check them out at the end of the day.

What are your key work hours today with breaks in between?

How did you manage distractions on phone/ email today?On average what was non- work related screen time today?

What physical activity or workout did you do today? Denote with mins or reps.

How much was spent out of pocket today? In what?

Was there any negotiation? Business, time and

family? Write down 2 amazing things about you or about the way you think.

What insecurities and negative feelings did you deal with today? How do you rationalize them for tomorrow?

Draw a diagram/ art / flowchart of your dreams today: use intuition

What are your before-bed affirmations for today?
Physical:
Emotional:
Social:

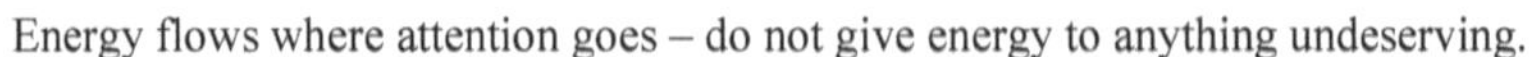

Spiritual:

One new psycho - spiritual learning from you today:

12 Self concept : Date:

What are your morning affirmations for today?

Physical:
Emotional:
Social:
Spiritual:

How well rested did you feel in the morning?

What are your plans, meetings, targets and non - negotiables for today? Check them out at the end of the day.

What are your key work hours today with breaks in between?

How did you manage distractions on phone/ email today?On average what was non- work related screen time today?

What physical activity or workout did you do today? Denote with mins or reps.

How much was spent out of pocket today? In what?

Was there any negotiation? Business, time and family? Write down 2 amazing things about you or about the way you think.

What insecurities and negative feelings did you deal with today? How do you rationalize them for tomorrow?

Draw a diagram/ art / flowchart of your dreams today: use intuition

What are your before-bed affirmations for today?
Physical:
Emotional:
Social:
Spiritual:

One new psycho - spiritual learning from you today:

13. Self concept : Date:

What are your morning affirmations for today?

Physical:
Emotional:
Social:
Spiritual:

How well rested did you feel in the morning?

What are your plans, meetings, targets and non - negotiables for today? Check them out at the end of the day.

What are your key work hours today with breaks in between?

How did you manage distractions on phone/ email today?On average what was non- work related screen time today?

What physical activity or workout did you do today? Denote with mins or reps.

How much was spent out of pocket today? In what?

Was there any negotiation? Business, time and family? Write down 2 amazing things about you or about the way you think.

What insecurities and negative feelings did you deal with today? How do you rationalize them for tomorrow?

Draw a diagram/ art / flowchart of your dreams today: use intuition

What are your before-bed affirmations for today?
Physical:
Emotional:
Social:
Spiritual:

One new psycho - spiritual learning from you today:

14. Self concept : Date:

What are your morning affirmations for today?

Physical:
Emotional:
Social:
Spiritual:

How well rested did you feel in the morning?

What are your plans, meetings, targets and non - negotiables for today? Check them out at the end of the day.

What are your key work hours today with breaks in between?

How did you manage distractions on phone/ email today?On average what was non- work related screen time today?

What physical activity or workout did you do today? Denote with mins or reps.

How much was spent out of pocket today? In what?

Was there any negotiation? Business, time and family? Write down 2 amazing things about you or about the way you think.

What insecurities and negative feelings did you deal with today? How do you rationalize them for tomorrow?

Draw a diagram/ art / flowchart of your dreams today: use intuition

What are your before-bed affirmations for today?
Physical:
Emotional:
Social:
Spiritual:

One new psycho - spiritual learning from you today:

15. Self concept : Date:

What are your morning affirmations for today?

Physical:
Emotional:
Social:
Spiritual:

How well rested did you feel in the morning?

What are your plans, meetings, targets and non - negotiables for today? Check them out at the end of the day.

What are your key work hours today with breaks in between?

How did you manage distractions on phone/ email today?On average what was non- work related screen time today?

What physical activity or workout did you do today? Denote with mins or reps.

How much was spent out of pocket today? In what?

Was there any negotiation? Business, time and family? Write down 2 amazing things about you or about the way you think.

What insecurities and negative feelings did you deal with today? How do you rationalize them for tomorrow?

Draw a diagram/ art / flowchart of your dreams

today: use intuition

What are your before-bed affirmations for today?
Physical:
Emotional:
Social:
Spiritual:

One new psycho - spiritual learning from you today:

16. Self concept : Date:

What are your morning affirmations for today?

Physical:
Emotional:
Social:
Spiritual:

How well rested did you feel in the morning?

What are your plans, meetings, targets and non - negotiables for today? Check them out at the end of the day.

What are your key work hours today with breaks in between?

How did you manage distractions on phone/ email today?On average what was non- work related screen time today?

What physical activity or workout did you do today? Denote with mins or reps.

How much was spent out of pocket today? In what?

Was there any negotiation? Business, time and family? Write down 2 amazing things about you or about the way you think.

What insecurities and negative feelings did you deal with today? How do you rationalize them for tomorrow?

Draw a diagram/ art / flowchart of your dreams today: use intuition

What are your before-bed affirmations for today?
Physical:
Emotional:
Social:
Spiritual:

One new psycho - spiritual learning from you today:

17. Self concept : Date:

What are your morning affirmations for today?

Physical:
Emotional:
Social:
Spiritual:

How well rested did you feel in the morning?

What are your plans, meetings, targets and non - negotiables for today? Check them out at the end of the day.

What are your key work hours today with breaks in between?

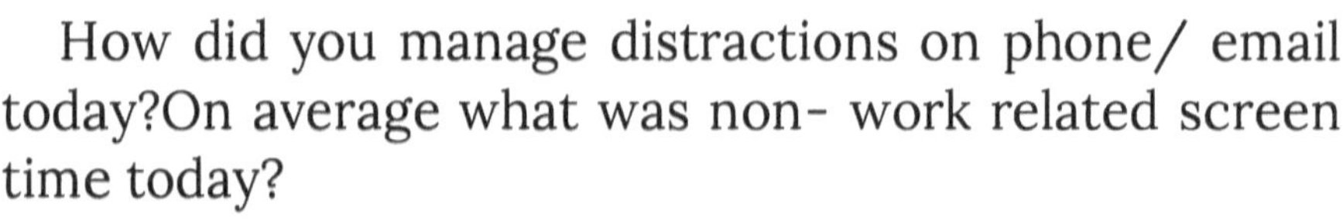

How did you manage distractions on phone/ email today?On average what was non- work related screen time today?

What physical activity or workout did you do today? Denote with mins or reps.

How much was spent out of pocket today? In what?

Was there any negotiation? Business, time and family? Write down 2 amazing things about you or about the way you think.

What insecurities and negative feelings did you deal

with today? How do you rationalize them for tomorrow?

Draw a diagram/ art / flowchart of your dreams today: use intuition

What are your before-bed affirmations for today?
Physical:
Emotional:
Social:
Spiritual:

One new psycho - spiritual learning from you today:

18 Self concept : Date:

What are your morning affirmations for today?

Physical:
Emotional:
Social:
Spiritual:

How well rested did you feel in the morning?

What are your plans, meetings, targets and non - negotiables for today? Check them out at the end of the day.

What are your key work hours today with breaks in between?

How did you manage distractions on phone/ email today?On average what was non- work related screen time today?

What physical activity or workout did you do today? Denote with mins or reps.

How much was spent out of pocket today? In what?

Was there any negotiation? Business, time and family? Write down 2 amazing things about you or about the way you think.

What insecurities and negative feelings did you deal with today? How do you rationalize them for tomorrow?

Draw a diagram/ art / flowchart of your dreams today: use intuition

What are your before-bed affirmations for today?
Physical:
Emotional:
Social:
Spiritual:

One new psycho - spiritual learning from you today:

19. Self concept : Date:

What are your morning affirmations for today?

Physical:
Emotional:
Social:
Spiritual:

How well rested did you feel in the morning?

What are your plans, meetings, targets and non - negotiables for today? Check them out at the end of the day.

What are your key work hours today with breaks in between?

How did you manage distractions on phone/ email today?On average what was non- work related screen time today?

What physical activity or workout did you do today? Denote with mins or reps.

How much was spent out of pocket today? In what?

Was there any negotiation? Business, time and family? Write down 2 amazing things about you or about the way you think.

What insecurities and negative feelings did you deal with today? How do you rationalize them for tomorrow?

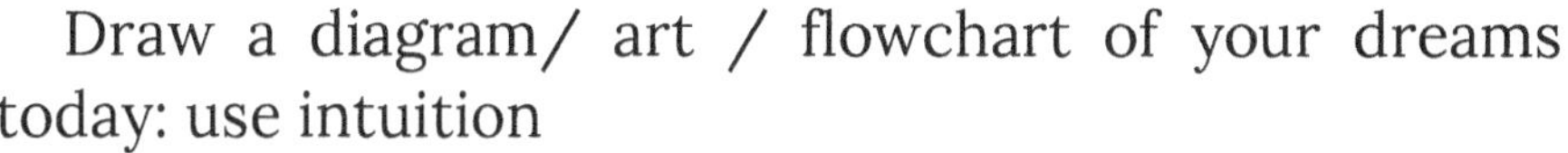

Draw a diagram/ art / flowchart of your dreams today: use intuition

What are your before-bed affirmations for today?
Physical:
Emotional:
Social:
Spiritual:

One new psycho - spiritual learning from you today:

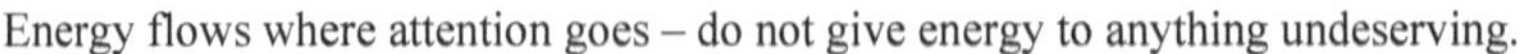

20. Self concept : Date:

What are your morning affirmations for today?

Physical:
Emotional:
Social:
Spiritual:

How well rested did you feel in the morning?

What are your plans, meetings, targets and non - negotiables for today? Check them out at the end of the day.

What are your key work hours today with breaks in between?

How did you manage distractions on phone/ email today?On average what was non- work related screen time today?

What physical activity or workout did you do today? Denote with mins or reps.

How much was spent out of pocket today? In what?

Was there any negotiation? Business, time and family? Write down 2 amazing things about you or about the way you think.

What insecurities and negative feelings did you deal with today? How do you rationalize them for tomorrow?

Draw a diagram/ art / flowchart of your dreams today: use intuition

What are your before-bed affirmations for today?
Physical:
Emotional:
Social:
Spiritual:

One new psycho - spiritual learning from you today:

21. Self concept : Date:

What are your morning affirmations for today?

Physical:
Emotional:
Social:
Spiritual:

How well rested did you feel in the morning?

What are your plans, meetings, targets and non - negotiables for today? Check them out at the end of the day.

What are your key work hours today with breaks in between?

How did you manage distractions on phone/ email today?On average what was non- work related screen time today?

What physical activity or workout did you do today? Denote with mins or reps.

How much was spent out of pocket today? In what?

Was there any negotiation? Business, time and family? Write down 2 amazing things about you or about the way you think.

What insecurities and negative feelings did you deal with today? How do you rationalize them for tomorrow?

Draw a diagram/ art / flowchart of your dreams today: use intuition

What are your before-bed affirmations for today?
Physical:
Emotional:
Social:
Spiritual:

One new psycho - spiritual learning from you today:

22. Self concept : Date:

What are your morning affirmations for today?

Physical:
Emotional:
Social:
Spiritual:

How well rested did you feel in the morning?

What are your plans, meetings, targets and non - negotiables for today? Check them out at the end of the day.

What are your key work hours today with breaks in between?

How did you manage distractions on phone/ email today?On average what was non- work related screen time today?

What physical activity or workout did you do today? Denote with mins or reps.

How much was spent out of pocket today? In what?

Was there any negotiation? Business, time and family? Write down 2 amazing things about you or about the way you think.

What insecurities and negative feelings did you deal with today? How do you rationalize them for tomorrow?

Draw a diagram/ art / flowchart of your dreams today: use intuition

What are your before-bed affirmations for today?
Physical:
Emotional:
Social:
Spiritual:

One new psycho - spiritual learning from you today:

23. Self concept : Date:

What are your morning affirmations for today?

Physical:
Emotional:
Social:
Spiritual:

How well rested did you feel in the morning?

What are your plans, meetings, targets and non -

negotiables for today? Check them out at the end of the day.

What are your key work hours today with breaks in between?

How did you manage distractions on phone/ email today?On average what was non- work related screen time today?

What physical activity or workout did you do today? Denote with mins or reps.

How much was spent out of pocket today? In what?

Was there any negotiation? Business, time and family? Write down 2 amazing things about you or about the way you think.

What insecurities and negative feelings did you deal with today? How do you rationalize them for tomorrow?

Draw a diagram/ art / flowchart of your dreams today: use intuition

What are your before-bed affirmations for today?
Physical:
Emotional:
Social:
Spiritual:

One new psycho - spiritual learning from you today:

24. Self concept : Date:

What are your morning affirmations for today?

Physical:
Emotional:
Social:
Spiritual:

How well rested did you feel in the morning?

What are your plans, meetings, targets and non - negotiables for today? Check them out at the end of the day.

What are your key work hours today with breaks in between?

How did you manage distractions on phone/ email today?On average what was non- work related screen time today?

What physical activity or workout did you do today? Denote with mins or reps.

How much was spent out of pocket today? In what?

Was there any negotiation? Business, time and family? Write down 2 amazing things about you or about the way you think.

What insecurities and negative feelings did you deal with today? How do you rationalize them for tomorrow?

Draw a diagram/ art / flowchart of your dreams today: use intuition

What are your before-bed affirmations for today?
Physical:
Emotional:
Social:
Spiritual:

One new psycho - spiritual learning from you today:

25. Self concept : Date:

What are your morning affirmations for today?

Physical:
Emotional:
Social:
Spiritual:

How well rested did you feel in the morning?

What are your plans, meetings, targets and non - negotiables for today? Check them out at the end of the day.

What are your key work hours today with breaks in between?

How did you manage distractions on phone/ email today?On average what was non- work related screen time today?

What physical activity or workout did you do today? Denote with mins or reps.

How much was spent out of pocket today? In what?

Was there any negotiation? Business, time and family? Write down 2 amazing things about you or about the way you think.

What insecurities and negative feelings did you deal with today? How do you rationalize them for tomorrow?

Draw a diagram/ art / flowchart of your dreams today: use intuition

What are your before-bed affirmations for today?
Physical:
Emotional:
Social:
Spiritual:

One new psycho - spiritual learning from you today:

26. Self concept : Date:

What are your morning affirmations for today?

Physical:
Emotional:
Social:
Spiritual:

How well rested did you feel in the morning?

What are your plans, meetings, targets and non - negotiables for today? Check them out at the end of the day.

What are your key work hours today with breaks in between?

How did you manage distractions on phone/ email today?On average what was non- work related screen time today?

What physical activity or workout did you do today? Denote with mins or reps.

How much was spent out of pocket today? In what?

Was there any negotiation? Business, time and family? Write down 2 amazing things about you or about the way you think.

What insecurities and negative feelings did you deal with today? How do you rationalize them for tomorrow?

Draw a diagram/ art / flowchart of your dreams today: use intuition

What are your before-bed affirmations for today?
Physical:
Emotional:
Social:
Spiritual:

One new psycho - spiritual learning from you today:

27. Self concept : Date:

What are your morning affirmations for today?

Physical:
Emotional:
Social:
Spiritual:

How well rested did you feel in the morning?

What are your plans, meetings, targets and non - negotiables for today? Check them out at the end of the day.

What are your key work hours today with breaks in between?

How did you manage distractions on phone/ email today?On average what was non- work related screen time today?

What physical activity or workout did you do today? Denote with mins or reps.

How much was spent out of pocket today? In what?

Was there any negotiation? Business, time and family? Write down 2 amazing things about you or about the way you think.

What insecurities and negative feelings did you deal

with today? How do you rationalize them for tomorrow?

Draw a diagram/ art / flowchart of your dreams today: use intuition

What are your before-bed affirmations for today?
Physical:
Emotional:
Social:

Spiritual:

One new psycho - spiritual learning from you today:

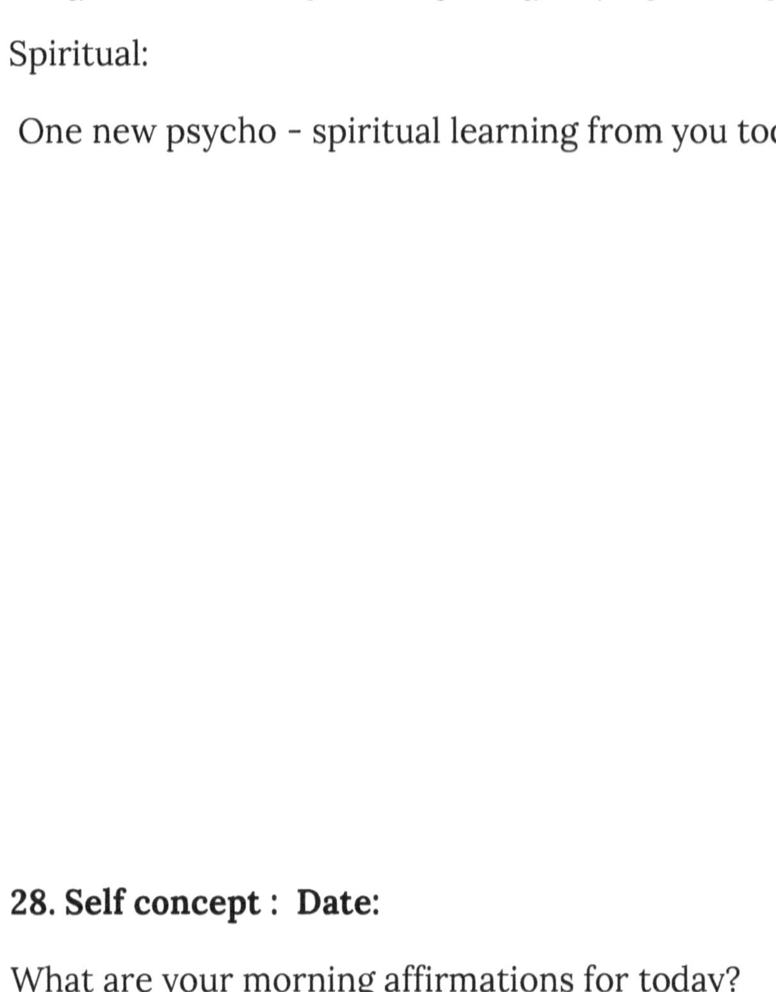

28. Self concept : Date:

What are your morning affirmations for today?

Physical:
Emotional:
Social:
Spiritual:

How well rested did you feel in the morning?

What are your plans, meetings, targets and non - negotiables for today? Check them out at the end of the day.

What are your key work hours today with breaks in between?

How did you manage distractions on phone/ email today?On average what was non- work related screen time today?

What physical activity or workout did you do today? Denote with mins or reps.

How much was spent out of pocket today? In what?

Was there any negotiation? Business, time and family? Write down 2 amazing things about you or about the way you think.

What insecurities and negative feelings did you deal

with today? How do you rationalize them for tomorrow?

Draw a diagram/ art / flowchart of your dreams today: use intuition

What are your before-bed affirmations for today?

Physical:
Emotional:
Social:
Spiritual:

One new psycho - spiritual learning from you today:

29. Self concept : Date:

What are your morning affirmations for today?

Physical:
Emotional:
Social:
Spiritual:

How well rested did you feel in the morning?

What are your plans, meetings, targets and non - negotiables for today? Check them out at the end of the day.

What are your key work hours today with breaks in between?

How did you manage distractions on phone/ email today?On average what was non- work related screen time today?

What physical activity or workout did you do today? Denote with mins or reps.

How much was spent out of pocket today? In what?

Was there any negotiation? Business, time and family? Write down 2 amazing things about you or about the way you think.

What insecurities and negative feelings did you deal

with today? How do you rationalize them for tomorrow?

Draw a diagram/ art / flowchart of your dreams today: use intuition

What are your before-bed affirmations for today?
Physical:
Emotional:
Social:
Spiritual:

One new psycho - spiritual learning from you today:

30. Self concept : Date:

What are your morning affirmations for today?

Physical:
Emotional:
Social:
Spiritual:

How well rested did you feel in the morning?

What are your plans, meetings, targets and non - negotiables for today? Check them out at the end of the day.

What are your key work hours today with breaks in between?

How did you manage distractions on phone/ email today?On average what was non- work related screen time today?

What physical activity or workout did you do today? Denote with mins or reps.

How much was spent out of pocket today? In what?

Was there any negotiation? Business, time and family? Write down 2 amazing things about you or about the way you think.

What insecurities and negative feelings did you deal

with today? How do you rationalize them for tomorrow?

Draw a diagram/ art / flowchart of your dreams today: use intuition

What are your before-bed affirmations for today?
Physical:
Emotional:
Social:
Spiritual:

One new psycho - spiritual learning from you today:

31. Self concept : Date:

What are your morning affirmations for today?

Physical:
Emotional:
Social:
Spiritual:

How well rested did you feel in the morning?

What are your plans, meetings, targets and non - negotiables for today? Check them out at the end of the day.

What are your key work hours today with breaks in between?

How did you manage distractions on phone/ email today?On average what was non- work related screen time today?

What physical activity or workout did you do today? Denote with mins or reps.

How much was spent out of pocket today? In what?

Was there any negotiation? Business, time and family? Write down 2 amazing things about you or about the way you think.

What insecurities and negative feelings did you deal

with today? How do you rationalize them for tomorrow?

Draw a diagram/ art / flowchart of your dreams today: use intuition

What are your before-bed affirmations for today?
Physical:
Emotional:
Social:
Spiritual:

One new psycho - spiritual learning from you today:

32. Self concept : Date:

What are your morning affirmations for today?

Physical:
Emotional:
Social:
Spiritual:

How well rested did you feel in the morning?

What are your plans, meetings, targets and non - negotiables for today? Check them out at the end of the day.

What are your key work hours today with breaks in between?

How did you manage distractions on phone/ email today?On average what was non- work related screen time today?

What physical activity or workout did you do today? Denote with mins or reps.

How much was spent out of pocket today? In what?

Was there any negotiation? Business, time and family? Write down 2 amazing things about you or about the way you think.

What insecurities and negative feelings did you deal with today? How do you rationalize them for tomorrow?

Draw a diagram/ art / flowchart of your dreams today: use intuition

What are your before-bed affirmations for today?
Physical:
Emotional:

Social:
Spiritual:

 One new psycho - spiritual learning from you today:

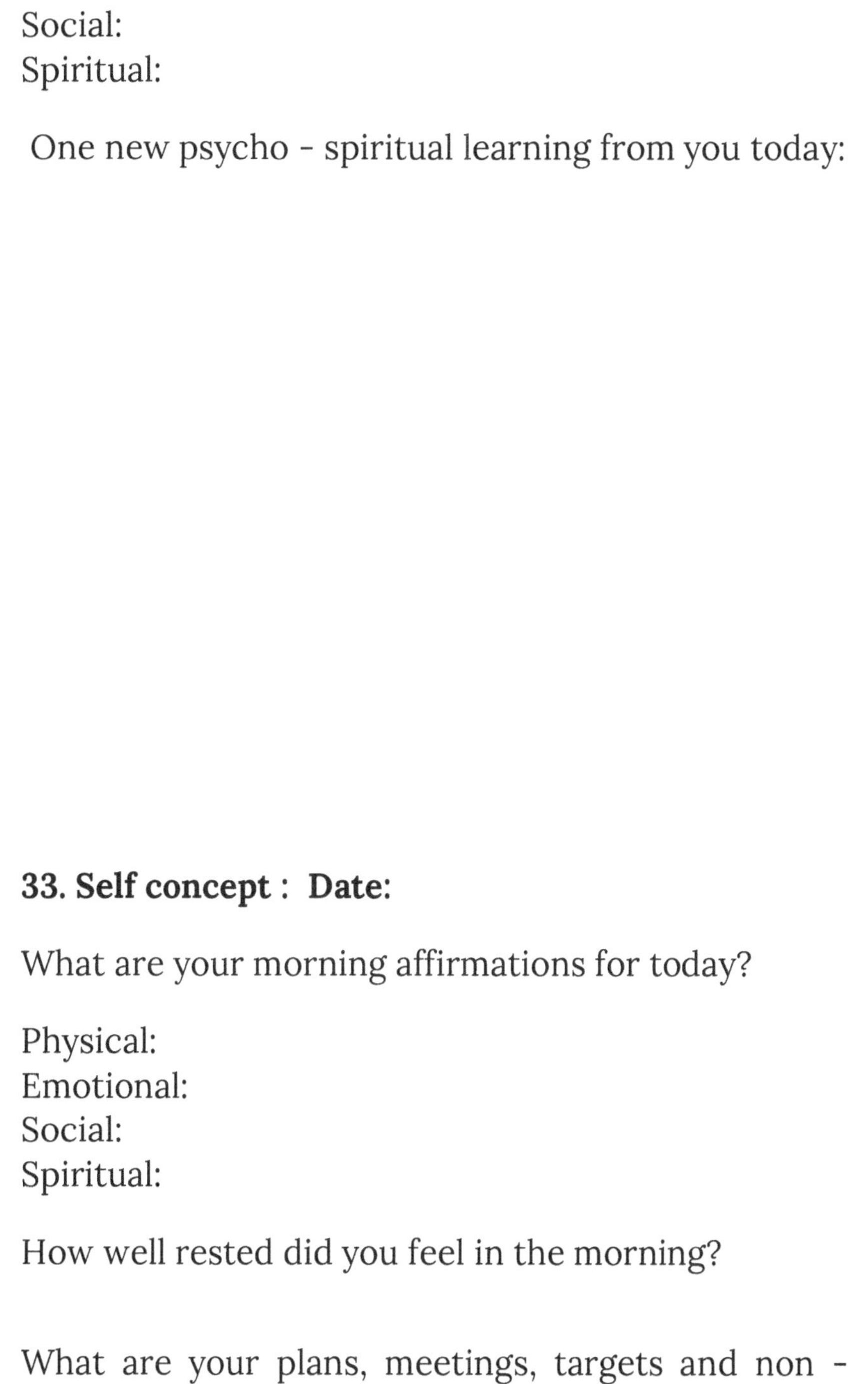

33. Self concept : Date:

What are your morning affirmations for today?

Physical:
Emotional:
Social:
Spiritual:

How well rested did you feel in the morning?

What are your plans, meetings, targets and non - negotiables for today? Check them out at the end of the day.

What are your key work hours today with breaks in between?

How did you manage distractions on phone/ email today?On average what was non- work related screen time today?

What physical activity or workout did you do today? Denote with mins or reps.

How much was spent out of pocket today? In what?

Was there any negotiation? Business, time and family? Write down 2 amazing things about you or about the way you think.

What insecurities and negative feelings did you deal with today? How do you rationalize them for tomorrow?

Draw a diagram/ art / flowchart of your dreams today: use intuition

What are your before-bed affirmations for today?

Physical:
Emotional:
Social:
Spiritual:

One new psycho - spiritual learning from you today:

34. Self concept : Date:

What are your morning affirmations for today?

Physical:
Emotional:
Social:
Spiritual:

How well rested did you feel in the morning?

What are your plans, meetings, targets and non - negotiables for today? Check them out at the end of the day.

What are your key work hours today with breaks in between?

How did you manage distractions on phone/ email today?On average what was non- work related screen time today?

What physical activity or workout did you do today? Denote with mins or reps.

How much was spent out of pocket today? In what?

Was there any negotiation? Business, time and family? Write down 2 amazing things about you or about the way you think.

What insecurities and negative feelings did you deal with today? How do you rationalize them for tomorrow?

Draw a diagram/ art / flowchart of your dreams today: use intuition

What are your before-bed affirmations for today?
Physical:
Emotional:
Social:
Spiritual:

One new psycho - spiritual learning from you today:

35. Self concept : Date:

What are your morning affirmations for today?

Physical:
Emotional:
Social:
Spiritual:

How well rested did you feel in the morning?

What are your plans, meetings, targets and non - negotiables for today? Check them out at the end of the day.

What are your key work hours today with breaks in between?

How did you manage distractions on phone/ email today?On average what was non- work related screen time today?

What physical activity or workout did you do today? Denote with mins or reps.

How much was spent out of pocket today? In what?

Was there any negotiation? Business, time and family? Write down 2 amazing things about you or about the way you think.

What insecurities and negative feelings did you deal with today? How do you rationalize them for tomorrow?

Draw a diagram/ art / flowchart of your dreams today: use intuition

What are your before-bed affirmations for today?
Physical:
Emotional:
Social:
Spiritual:

One new psycho - spiritual learning from you today:

36. Self concept : Date:

What are your morning affirmations for today?

Physical:
Emotional:
Social:
Spiritual:

How well rested did you feel in the morning?

What are your plans, meetings, targets and non - negotiables for today? Check them out at the end of the day.

What are your key work hours today with breaks in between?

How did you manage distractions on phone/ email today?On average what was non- work related screen time today?

What physical activity or workout did you do today? Denote with mins or reps.

How much was spent out of pocket today? In what?

Was there any negotiation? Business, time and family? Write down 2 amazing things about you or about the way you think.

What insecurities and negative feelings did you deal with today? How do you rationalize them for tomorrow?

Draw a diagram/ art / flowchart of your dreams today: use intuition

What are your before-bed affirmations for today?
Physical:
Emotional:
Social:
Spiritual:

One new psycho - spiritual learning from you today:

37. Self concept : Date:

What are your morning affirmations for today?

Physical:
Emotional:
Social:
Spiritual:

How well rested did you feel in the morning?

What are your plans, meetings, targets and non - negotiables for today? Check them out at the end of the

day.

What are your key work hours today with breaks in between?

How did you manage distractions on phone/ email today?On average what was non- work related screen time today?

What physical activity or workout did you do today? Denote with mins or reps.

How much was spent out of pocket today? In what?

Was there any negotiation? Business, time and family? Write down 2 amazing things about you or about the way you think.

What insecurities and negative feelings did you deal with today? How do you rationalize them for tomorrow?

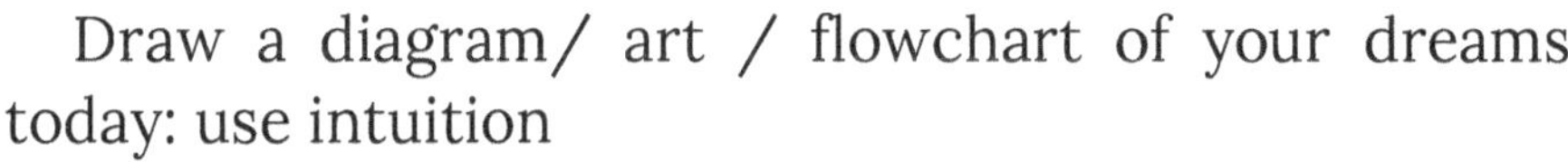

Draw a diagram/ art / flowchart of your dreams today: use intuition

What are your before-bed affirmations for today?
Physical:
Emotional:
Social:
Spiritual:

One new psycho - spiritual learning from you today:

38. Self concept : Date:

What are your morning affirmations for today?

Physical:
Emotional:
Social:
Spiritual:

How well rested did you feel in the morning?

What are your plans, meetings, targets and non - negotiables for today? Check them out at the end of the day.

What are your key work hours today with breaks in between?

How did you manage distractions on phone/ email today?On average what was non- work related screen time today?

What physical activity or workout did you do today? Denote with mins or reps.

How much was spent out of pocket today? In what?

Was there any negotiation? Business, time and family? Write down 2 amazing things about you or about the way you think.

What insecurities and negative feelings did you deal with today? How do you rationalize them for tomorrow?

Draw a diagram/ art / flowchart of your dreams today: use intuition

What are your before-bed affirmations for today?
Physical:
Emotional:
Social:
Spiritual:

One new psycho - spiritual learning from you today:

39. Self concept : Date:

What are your morning affirmations for today?

Physical:
Emotional:
Social:
Spiritual:

How well rested did you feel in the morning?

What are your plans, meetings, targets and non - negotiables for today? Check them out at the end of the day.

What are your key work hours today with breaks in between?

How did you manage distractions on phone/ email today?On average what was non- work related screen time today?

What physical activity or workout did you do today? Denote with mins or reps.

How much was spent out of pocket today? In what?

Was there any negotiation? Business, time and family? Write down 2 amazing things about you or about the way you think.

What insecurities and negative feelings did you deal with today? How do you rationalize them for tomorrow?

Draw a diagram/ art / flowchart of your dreams today: use intuition

What are your before-bed affirmations for today?
Physical:
Emotional:
Social:
Spiritual:

One new psycho - spiritual learning from you today:

40. Self concept : Date:

What are your morning affirmations for today?

Physical:
Emotional:
Social:
Spiritual:

How well rested did you feel in the morning?

What are your plans, meetings, targets and non - negotiables for today? Check them out at the end of the day.

What are your key work hours today with breaks in between?

How did you manage distractions on phone/ email today?On average what was non- work related screen time today?

What physical activity or workout did you do today? Denote with mins or reps.

How much was spent out of pocket today? In what?

Was there any negotiation? Business, time and family? Write down 2 amazing things about you or about the way you think.

What insecurities and negative feelings did you deal with today? How do you rationalize them for tomorrow?

Draw a diagram/ art / flowchart of your dreams today: use intuition

What are your before-bed affirmations for today?
Physical:
Emotional:
Social:
Spiritual:

One new psycho - spiritual learning from you today:

Energy flows where attention goes – do not give energy to anything undeserving.

41. Self concept : Date:

What are your morning affirmations for today?

Physical:
Emotional:
Social:
Spiritual:

How well rested did you feel in the morning?

What are your plans, meetings, targets and non - negotiables for today? Check them out at the end of the day.

What are your key work hours today with breaks in between?

How did you manage distractions on phone/ email today?On average what was non- work related screen time today?

What physical activity or workout did you do today? Denote with mins or reps.

How much was spent out of pocket today? In what?

Was there any negotiation? Business, time and family? Write down 2 amazing things about you or about the way you think.

What insecurities and negative feelings did you deal with today? How do you rationalize them for tomorrow?

Draw a diagram/ art / flowchart of your dreams today: use intuition

What are your before-bed affirmations for today?
Physical:
Emotional:
Social:
Spiritual:

One new psycho - spiritual learning from you today:

42. Self concept : Date:

What are your morning affirmations for today?

Physical:
Emotional:
Social:
Spiritual:

How well rested did you feel in the morning?

What are your plans, meetings, targets and non - negotiables for today? Check them out at the end of the

day.

What are your key work hours today with breaks in between?

How did you manage distractions on phone/ email today?On average what was non- work related screen time today?

What physical activity or workout did you do today? Denote with mins or reps.

How much was spent out of pocket today? In what?

Was there any negotiation? Business, time and family? Write down 2 amazing things about you or about the way you think.

What insecurities and negative feelings did you deal with today? How do you rationalize them for tomorrow?

Draw a diagram/ art / flowchart of your dreams today: use intuition

What are your before-bed affirmations for today?
Physical:
Emotional:
Social:
Spiritual:

One new psycho - spiritual learning from you today:

43. Self concept : Date:

What are your morning affirmations for today?

Physical:
Emotional:
Social:
Spiritual:

How well rested did you feel in the morning?

What are your plans, meetings, targets and non - negotiables for today? Check them out at the end of the day.

What are your key work hours today with breaks in between?

How did you manage distractions on phone/ email today?On average what was non- work related screen time today?

What physical activity or workout did you do today? Denote with mins or reps.

How much was spent out of pocket today? In what?

Was there any negotiation? Business, time and family? Write down 2 amazing things about you or about the way you think.

What insecurities and negative feelings did you deal with today? How do you rationalize them for tomorrow?

Draw a diagram/ art / flowchart of your dreams today: use intuition

What are your before-bed affirmations for today?
Physical:
Emotional:
Social:
Spiritual:

One new psycho - spiritual learning from you today:

44. Self concept : Date:

What are your morning affirmations for today?

Physical:
Emotional:
Social:
Spiritual:

How well rested did you feel in the morning?

What are your plans, meetings, targets and non - negotiables for today? Check them out at the end of the

day.

What are your key work hours today with breaks in between?

How did you manage distractions on phone/ email today?On average what was non- work related screen time today?

What physical activity or workout did you do today? Denote with mins or reps.

How much was spent out of pocket today? In what?

Was there any negotiation? Business, time and family? Write down 2 amazing things about you or about the way you think.

What insecurities and negative feelings did you deal with today? How do you rationalize them for tomorrow?

Draw a diagram/ art / flowchart of your dreams today: use intuition

What are your before-bed affirmations for today?
Physical:
Emotional:
Social:
Spiritual:

One new psycho - spiritual learning from you today:

45. Self concept : Date:

What are your morning affirmations for today?

Physical:
Emotional:
Social:
Spiritual:

How well rested did you feel in the morning?

What are your plans, meetings, targets and non - negotiables for today? Check them out at the end of the

day.

What are your key work hours today with breaks in between?

How did you manage distractions on phone/ email today?On average what was non- work related screen time today?

What physical activity or workout did you do today? Denote with mins or reps.

How much was spent out of pocket today? In what?

Was there any negotiation? Business, time and family? Write down 2 amazing things about you or about the way you think.

What insecurities and negative feelings did you deal with today? How do you rationalize them for tomorrow?

Draw a diagram/ art / flowchart of your dreams today: use intuition

What are your before-bed affirmations for today?
Physical:
Emotional:
Social:
Spiritual:

One new psycho - spiritual learning from you today:

46. Self concept : Date:

What are your morning affirmations for today?

Physical:
Emotional:
Social:
Spiritual:

How well rested did you feel in the morning?

What are your plans, meetings, targets and non -

negotiables for today? Check them out at the end of the day.

What are your key work hours today with breaks in between?

How did you manage distractions on phone/ email today?On average what was non- work related screen time today?

What physical activity or workout did you do today? Denote with mins or reps.

How much was spent out of pocket today? In what?

Was there any negotiation? Business, time and family? Write down 2 amazing things about you or about the way you think.

What insecurities and negative feelings did you deal with today? How do you rationalize them for tomorrow?

Draw a diagram/ art / flowchart of your dreams today: use intuition

What are your before-bed affirmations for today?
Physical:
Emotional:
Social:

Spiritual:

 One new psycho - spiritual learning from you today:

47. Self concept : Date:

What are your morning affirmations for today?

Physical:
Emotional:
Social:
Spiritual:

How well rested did you feel in the morning?

What are your plans, meetings, targets and non - negotiables for today? Check them out at the end of the day.

What are your key work hours today with breaks in between?

How did you manage distractions on phone/ email today?On average what was non- work related screen time today?

What physical activity or workout did you do today? Denote with mins or reps.

How much was spent out of pocket today? In what?

Was there any negotiation? Business, time and

family? Write down 2 amazing things about you or about the way you think.

What insecurities and negative feelings did you deal with today? How do you rationalize them for tomorrow?

Draw a diagram/ art / flowchart of your dreams today: use intuition

What are your before-bed affirmations for today?
Physical:
Emotional:
Social:
Spiritual:

One new psycho - spiritual learning from you today:

Energy flows where attention goes – do not give energy to anything undeserving.

48. Self concept : Date:

What are your morning affirmations for today?

Physical:
Emotional:
Social:
Spiritual:

How well rested did you feel in the morning?

What are your plans, meetings, targets and non - negotiables for today? Check them out at the end of the day.

What are your key work hours today with breaks in between?

How did you manage distractions on phone/ email today?On average what was non- work related screen time today?

What physical activity or workout did you do today? Denote with mins or reps.

How much was spent out of pocket today? In what?

Was there any negotiation? Business, time and family? Write down 2 amazing things about you or about the way you think.

What insecurities and negative feelings did you deal with today? How do you rationalize them for tomorrow?

Draw a diagram/ art / flowchart of your dreams today: use intuition

What are your before-bed affirmations for today?
Physical:
Emotional:
Social:
Spiritual:

One new psycho - spiritual learning from you today:

49. Self concept : Date:

What are your morning affirmations for today?

Physical:
Emotional:
Social:
Spiritual:

How well rested did you feel in the morning?

What are your plans, meetings, targets and non - negotiables for today? Check them out at the end of the day.

What are your key work hours today with breaks in between?

How did you manage distractions on phone/ email today?On average what was non- work related screen time today?

What physical activity or workout did you do today? Denote with mins or reps.

How much was spent out of pocket today? In what?

Was there any negotiation? Business, time and family? Write down 2 amazing things about you or about the way you think.

What insecurities and negative feelings did you deal with today? How do you rationalize them for tomorrow?

Draw a diagram/ art / flowchart of your dreams today: use intuition

What are your before-bed affirmations for today?
Physical:
Emotional:
Social:
Spiritual:

One new psycho - spiritual learning from you today:

50. Self concept : Date:

What are your morning affirmations for today?

Physical:
Emotional:
Social:
Spiritual:

How well rested did you feel in the morning?

What are your plans, meetings, targets and non - negotiables for today? Check them out at the end of the day.

What are your key work hours today with breaks in between?

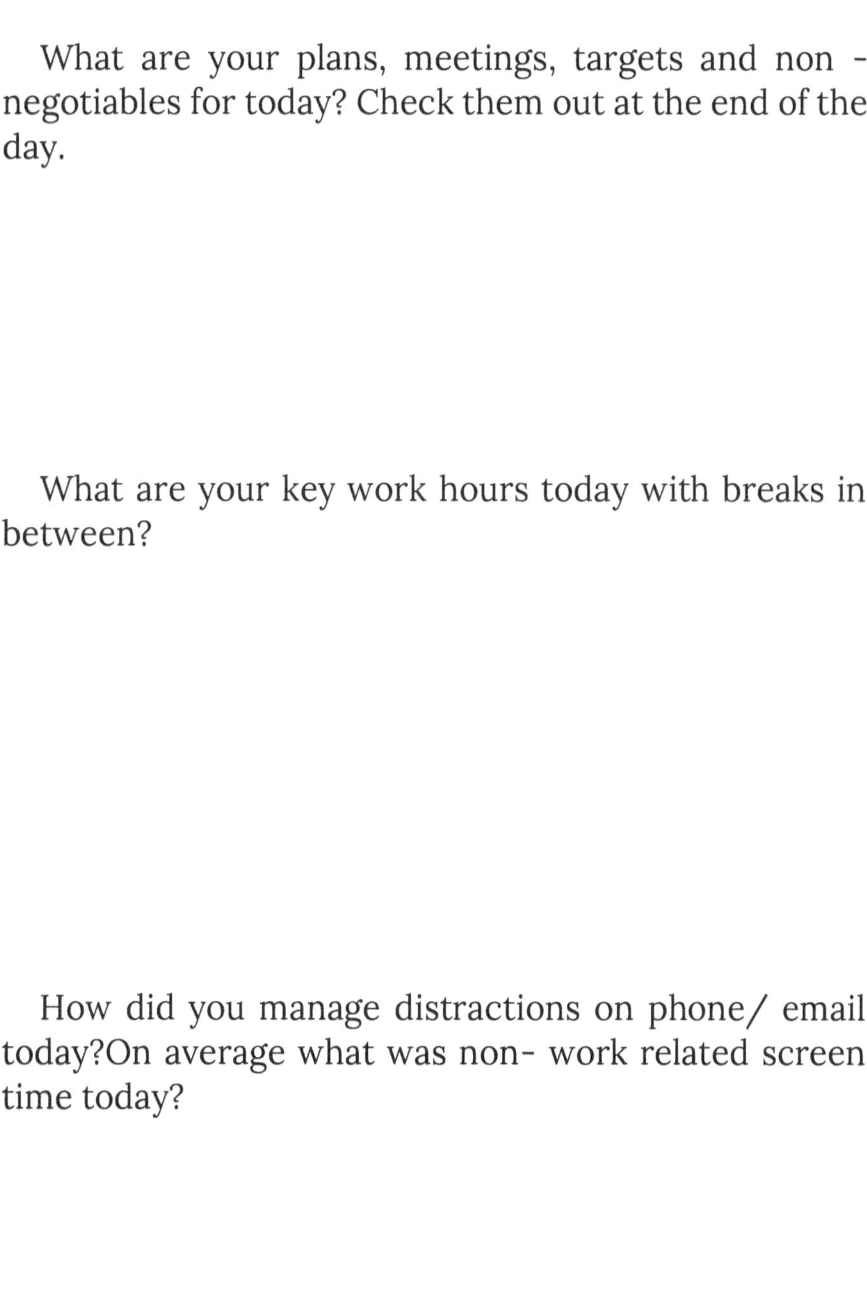

How did you manage distractions on phone/ email today?On average what was non- work related screen time today?

What physical activity or workout did you do today? Denote with mins or reps.

How much was spent out of pocket today? In what?

Was there any negotiation? Business, time and family? Write down 2 amazing things about you or about the way you think.

What insecurities and negative feelings did you deal with today? How do you rationalize them for tomorrow?

Draw a diagram/ art / flowchart of your dreams today: use intuition

What are your before-bed affirmations for today?
Physical:
Emotional:
Social:
Spiritual:

One new psycho - spiritual learning from you today:

51. Self concept : Date:

What are your morning affirmations for today?

Physical:
Emotional:
Social:
Spiritual:

How well rested did you feel in the morning?

What are your plans, meetings, targets and non - negotiables for today? Check them out at the end of the day.

What are your key work hours today with breaks in between?

How did you manage distractions on phone/ email today?On average what was non- work related screen time today?

What physical activity or workout did you do today? Denote with mins or reps.

How much was spent out of pocket today? In what?

Was there any negotiation? Business, time and family? Write down 2 amazing things about you or about the way you think.

What insecurities and negative feelings did you deal with today? How do you rationalize them for tomorrow?

Draw a diagram/ art / flowchart of your dreams today: use intuition

What are your before-bed affirmations for today?
Physical:
Emotional:
Social:
Spiritual:

One new psycho - spiritual learning from you today:

52. . Self concept : Date:

What are your morning affirmations for today?

Physical:
Emotional:
Social:
Spiritual:

How well rested did you feel in the morning?

What are your plans, meetings, targets and non - negotiables for today? Check them out at the end of the day.

What are your key work hours today with breaks in between?

How did you manage distractions on phone/ email today?On average what was non- work related screen time today?

What physical activity or workout did you do today? Denote with mins or reps.

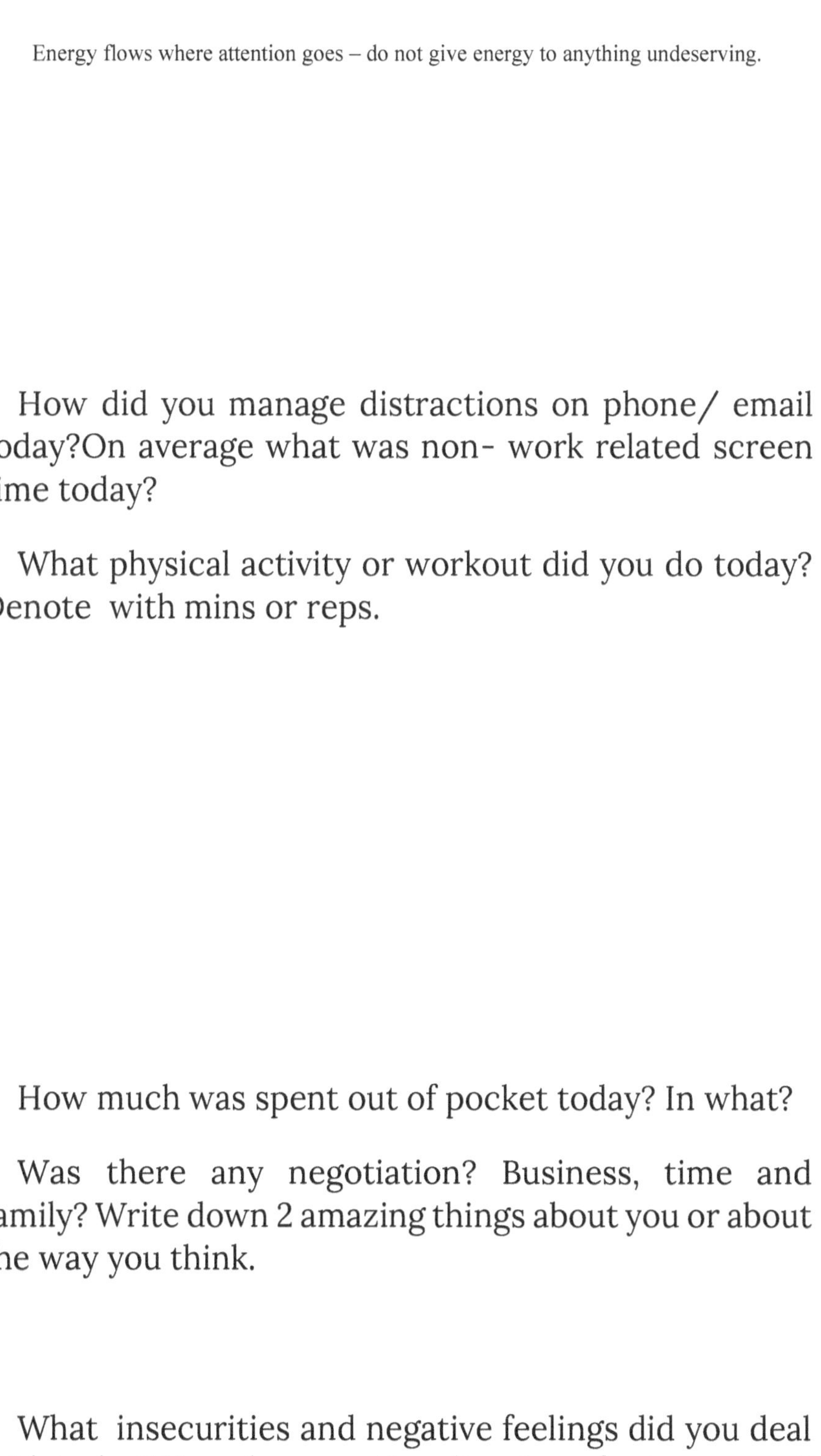

How much was spent out of pocket today? In what?

Was there any negotiation? Business, time and family? Write down 2 amazing things about you or about the way you think.

What insecurities and negative feelings did you deal with today? How do you rationalize them for tomorrow?

Draw a diagram/ art / flowchart of your dreams today: use intuition

What are your before-bed affirmations for today?
Physical:
Emotional:
Social:
Spiritual:

One new psycho - spiritual learning from you today:

Month 1 : let's hear you describe your life vision and how you see your future self. What is the most grateful thing to you this month?

Month 2 : How do you view your life with abundance in every aspect? what abundance do you believe you deserve? What do you think you will be grateful for in the future?

Month 3 : How does your routine for everyday fit into your future self and the empire you are building? Describe in few words what have you dropped or left to get to this place? What makes must you let go?

Fear or faith, it can only be one.
Both are a decision to believe in the unseen.

-Coach Karan, Manifesting Better

The more I tried changing the world, the less it did, the more I changed myself, the more it changed as a reflection.

-Coach Karan, Manifesting Better

Energy flows where attention goes – do not give energy to anything undeserving.

Silence is the most powerful path to greatness.

- David Ghiyam

If you have a desire to be great, it means it is in your destiny one day to be great. However, your job is to LET THAT GO and do the spiritual work.

- David Ghiyam

Kabbalah explains we must have affinity of form with the Source, the Creator, in order to access the realm of miracles.

- David Ghiyam

Visualisation:

Imagine the chart below as a visual representation of your overall growth for the next year.

Jot down or draw/ doodle what all need to be addressed and very well can be addressed.

Energy flows where attention goes – do not give energy to anything undeserving.

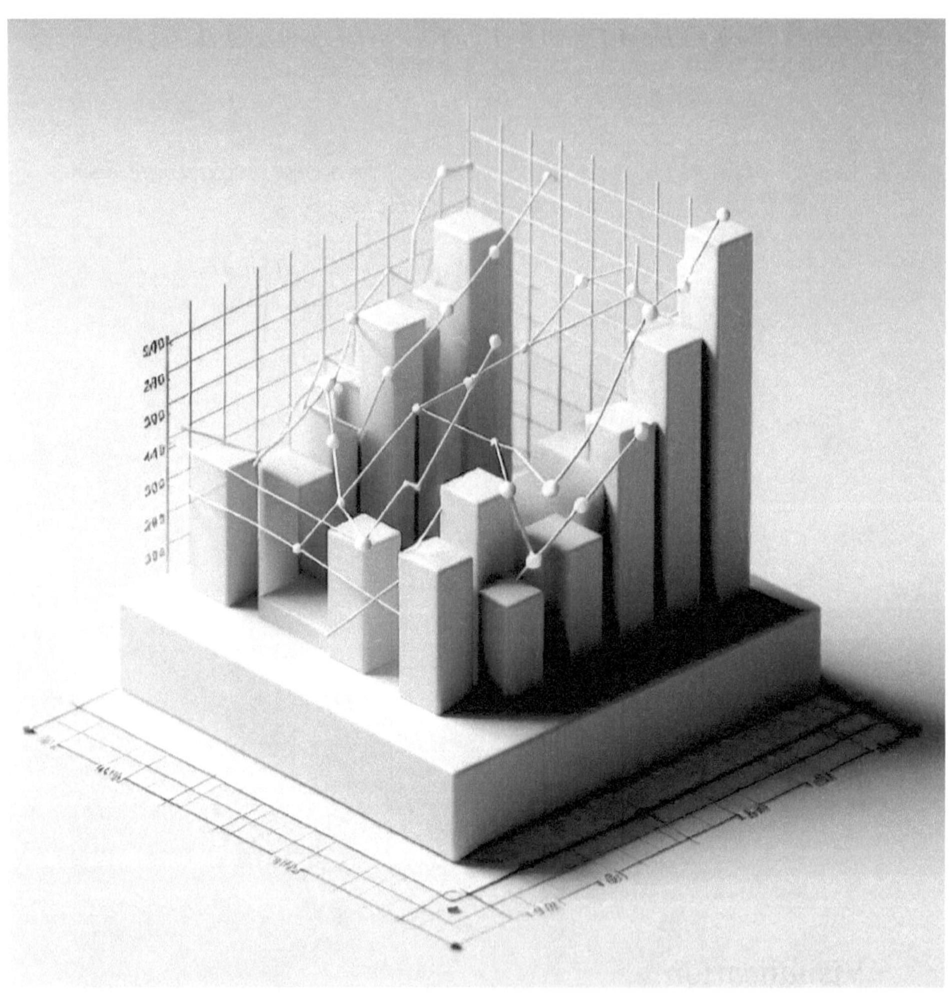

Energy flows where attention goes – do not give energy to anything undeserving.

*Many thanks to one of **the most amazing people** making the world go round.*

We are very grateful to you for making us a part of your journey of attracting what you already deserve.

Thank you for being an invaluable client.

We hope to serve your journey better.

- Team Floating Sandclock,
Always rooting for you.

Let's review your ambience:

1. Does the lighting in your workspace affect your ability to concentrate?

2. Do you prefer a cooler or warmer temperature in your work environment for optimal focus?

3. Would you say you're more productive immediately after waking up or after completing a morning workout/ getting ready for work?

Energy flows where attention goes – do not give energy to anything undeserving.

4. How many minutes of break do you take during your workday, and how do they impact your focus?

5. At what time of day do you typically feel most alert and focused?

6. How do you usually feel before and *after meals* in terms of your ability to concentrate?

Energy flows where attention goes – do not give energy to anything undeserving.

7. Can you maintain focus without hours without the consumption of caffeinated beverages like coffee or tea?

8. When someone interrupts you during a conversation or task, how long does it typically take for you to regain focus? Answer in minutes.

9. What type of background noise, if any, helps you concentrate the most (e.g., white noise, instrumental music)?

Energy flows where attention goes – do not give energy to anything undeserving.

10. How do you structure your workspace to minimize distractions and enhance focus?

11. Do you prefer natural or artificial light in your workspace, and how does it impact your productivity?

12. How do you manage interruptions from colleagues or notifications on your devices while working?

Energy flows where attention goes – do not give energy to anything undeserving.

13. What role does air quality play in your ability to focus and remain productive throughout the day? Do you get distracted by smells?

14. Are there specific ergonomic features or equipment in your workspace that you find essential for focus?

15. How do you prioritize tasks to ensure you're focusing on the most important activities first?

Energy flows where attention goes – do not give energy to anything undeserving.

16. Do you have a specific routine or ritual that helps you transition into a focused work mindset?

17. How do you handle stress or overwhelm during busy periods to prevent burnout?

18. Are there any specific foods that you find enhance your concentration and energy levels?

Energy flows where attention goes – do not give energy to anything undeserving.

19. What strategies do you use to maintain focus and productivity during longer work sessions or projects?

20. What time do you wind down and relax after a productive workday? Do you like to be around people when you do that?

21. Interacting with whom drains you for the rest of your workday?

Energy flows where attention goes – do not give energy to anything undeserving.

22. What steps have you taken to minimize or completely avoid your interaction with this person?

23. Are there certain practices or any routine practised in perfect order without which you cannot complete your work efficiently?

Energy flows where attention goes – do not give energy to anything undeserving.

24. What device-care practices do you implement each day?

25. Are there ways to optimise your internet usage and/or reduce the bill?

More programming for you…..write down how you will implement this in your daily life with a realistic scenario

"Focus is the gateway to success. When your mind is laser-focused on your goals, nothing can deter you from achieving them." - Vishen Lakhiani

"In the alpha brain state, you tap into your creative potential and unlock the power of your subconscious mind to manifest your desires." - Joe Dispenza

"The delta brain state is where true transformation occurs, rewiring your neural pathways for lasting change and personal growth." - Bruce Lipton

"Energy is the currency of the universe. When you align your energy with your desires, you become a magnet for manifestation." - Nassim Haramein

Energy flows where attention goes – do not give energy to anything undeserving.

"Your conscious mind sets the intention, but it's your subconscious mind that holds the key to unlocking your full potential." - Napoleon Hill

"Success is not about luck or circumstance; it's about cultivating the right habits and mindset to overcome obstacles and achieve your goals." - Jack Ma

"Resilience is not the absence of adversity but the ability to bounce back stronger than before, turning challenges into opportunities for growth." - Vishen Lakhiani

"Time is your most valuable asset. Invest it wisely in activities that align with your goals and values." - James Murphy

"The law of attraction is always at work, whether you realize it or not. What you focus on expands, so choose your thoughts wisely." - Joe Dispenza

Energy flows where attention goes – do not give energy to anything undeserving.

"Life is a matrix of infinite possibilities. When you shift your perspective, you unlock new realities and opportunities for abundance." - Nassim Haramein

"Your identity is not fixed; it's fluid and can be shaped by your beliefs, habits, and actions. Embrace the power of identity shifting to become the person you want to be." - Vishen Lakhiani

"Focus on the journey, not the destination. Success is not a destination but a continuous process of growth and self-discovery." - Usain Bolt (hint: describe how repeated effort is necessary)

"The subconscious mind is like a garden. Plant seeds of positivity and watch as your thoughts blossom into reality." - Napoleon Hill

Energy flows where attention goes – do not give energy to anything undeserving.

"Success is the result of daily habits compounded over time. It's not about big leaps but small consistent actions that lead to extraordinary results." - Jack Ma

"Resilience is the art of facing adversity with courage and grace, knowing that every setback is an opportunity for growth." - Joe Dispenza

"Time is a precious gift. Don't waste it on things that don't align with your purpose or bring you joy." - Steve Jobs

"The law of attraction operates on the principle of like attracts like. Align your thoughts, emotions, and actions with your desires, and watch as the universe conspires to manifest them." - Vishen Lakhiani

Energy flows where attention goes – do not give energy to anything undeserving.

"Life is not predetermined; it's what you make of it. Take control of your destiny and create the life you desire." - Bruce Lipton

"Your subconscious mind is the powerhouse of your beliefs and behaviors. By reprogramming it, you can create new patterns of success and abundance." - Napoleon Hill

"Habits are the invisible architects of your life. Choose them wisely, for they will determine your destiny." - James Murphy

Energy flows where attention goes – do not give energy to anything undeserving.

"Resilience is not about avoiding failure but learning from it and using it as a stepping stone to success." - Jack Ma

"Time is the most valuable asset we have. It's not about how much time we have, but how we choose to spend it." - Joe Dispenza

"The law of attraction is a powerful force that operates in the universe. By aligning your thoughts and emotions with your desires, you can attract anything you want into your life." - Napoleon Hill

Energy flows where attention goes – do not give energy to anything undeserving.

"Life is a matrix of infinite possibilities. When you tap into the power of your subconscious mind, you can create the reality you desire." - Vishen Lakhiani

"Success is not about luck or talent; it's about mindset and perseverance. With the right attitude and work ethic, anything is possible." - Usain Bolt

Our philosophy:

No two journeys are the same and so we believe in individualistic transformation. Hence our segmentation of our customers into The Doer, The Innovator and The Hustler. At each stage of life an individual might be undergoing different experiences and their interests or action plans might lean towards one of the above types/ archetypes, whatever you might like to call them. We strongly believe and care for the mental, emotional and financial wellness of our clients and have taken immense care to help them focus on all three. You might use this journal as you like and at any time of the year. We believe in continuous improvement because that's just the way it is!

We welcome any feedback to be written to:
floatingsandclock@gmail.com.

Thanks.

Vision board 1:

Vision board 2:

Vision board 3: